# COW MIRE SONGS

## SHELBY STEPHENSON

**Cushing Publishing**
www.cushingpublishing.com

Copyright @2023 Shelby Stephenson
ISBN: 979-8-9889575-2-2

Cushing Publishing
P.O. Box 38
Middlesex, NC 27557

Cover Design Qarol Price
Cover Photo Yanna Slutskaya

*for Nin*

# ACKNOWLEDGMENTS

*Active Muse: A Journal of Literature, Poetry, and Art*: "A Clock: Our Arms"

*After the Storm: A Poetry and Prose Anthology*: "Guns."

*Agapanthus*: "Storms," "March," "Raccoon Sunning"

*The Bookends Review*: "Trying to Get to the Bottom of It"

*Fleas on the Dog*: "Possum to the Fleas," "Memory," "North America's Only Native Marsupial," "The Man Seeking Water Lets the Water-Witcher Hold the Vine,"

"Pantoum for Oliver"

*Heron X Clan*: "The Mule Gray" *Hole in the Head Review*: "The Territorial Basset"

*K'in*: "Of Childhood's Groves of Pastures"

*Lothlorien Poetry Journal*: *Sentient Souls* : "Banjo-Head"

*Meat for Two: The Valley Review*: "Letters to Fred Chappell"

*Sandhills*: "The Leaning Basketball Pole"

*Sparks of Calliope*: "Gone Fishing"

*Speckled Trout Review*: "Audrey, Afterwards," "Hank, During, and Afterwards"

*Synchronized Chaos*: "Channel Cat," "Blistered," "Libby Campbell," "Independence," "Love Works"

*A Wreath of Golden Laurels*: "Elvis"

# Table of Contents

# FOR MERRILL LEFFLER

You open the closet door among the rhythms
and pull your father's accordion out. The timing
is exacting. A cow wallows in a meadow
through the window. Her calf nibbles daises on
the way to nuzzle its mother far from the whizz
of Sanders Road. The pull-cords dangle in the
Plankhouse, the three rooms and pantry expanding
the bellows of the accordion you place back
on the shelf. I'm remembering when Hank died.
My world stopped under the walnut tree as I heard
the announcer's heartsickness over the vibrations.

# MEMORY

Try lingerie rather than linguistics.
Or if you are looking for Truth, a climax works,
Though prompt the letters me to stop
Where Level Cross keeps Randolph County
Safe for a racecar (racecar).

I'm not palindroming anything
I know better than pop, for I am helpless
As a kitten on a spree, a free agent
Of sorts, crying for someone to put my socks away
In a drawer in a bureau I got
At St. Vincent de Paul decades ago,
An eight-drawer, certainly an antique,
For it's dressed with wheels and pizzazz!

Let the mules go free! Sure, they'll find themselves.
The reins shall go limp, the manes flow,
The wind shape music in the breaking wind.
Notice I am cautious of saying, "fart," for it jumps
The lines and makes a meadow for the smell like camphor
Or some pitch tarring the mindful forest
Full of mime-fields and dirty shoes.

There is no ambiguity here, no guide
To take you home or poet to hum
A song, maybe smell a scene or three,
Though once, when I was a lad,
My race filled with white parts of chicken manures.

Arrivederci: I have seen that yard before.
Your map is good as mine: Pam is a nice dubiety.

8

# SHELBY STEPHENSON

She does not turn redder when she solos as Pamela.

# A CLOCK: OUR ARMS

We kissed under the clock that cold March night,
Though memory does not allow recall,
And both our arms clung to the curfew's fall;
      They seemed all hands to me, a singing sight.

Your eyes were closed to me the way you see
Inside instinct pure as ditties I learned,
While Mac ran, Muff climbed a tree; Humpty leaned
      And lost the lasting promises of glee.

You were anxious to get to your dorm room
Without being grounded by dalliance;
I joined John in his Plymouth Valiant.
      He looked charming as any future groom.

Looking back, please know that he took his bride
And I studied the law as it failed me;
Your face's profile eased the clock and tree.
      The story edges our love's lasting guide.

## HEART

When I feel the pulsing wrist,
      Ankle or heart of the mulberry tree,
      My head seems to question
Why my mother's father dangles in my thirst.

His face is dull, white, and torn,
      As though worries weigh
      Him down, allowing his toes
To touch the frozen dirt at morn.

In his eyes the bulges stare,
      As if being done in
      Becomes too far gone to breathe –
"Mama, mama, I heard him swear!

"Lord God Almighty,
      The rest I hear bends
      The limb, though not enough to bring
Him down to me."

So Orron spoke in opposition
      To what he saw, his pains,
      Seeing his father's remains
In deathly position.

I cannot surmise his mom's response;
      I, her grandson, do not understand
      How Bad gorges Good,
To stop the heart's beating loss.

The living's end, I cannot say

# COW MIRE SONGS

What the boy, my uncle, saw
That cold February day
When Marshall Perry Johnson danced his life away.

# OF CHILDHOOD'S GROVES FOR PASTURES

Groves, the knife-shaped blades of grass,
Times I have felt myself fall over castles

In Cow Mire, the chapel of wisteria
Where I swung as a boy too far from the city

To afford more than the turn of seasons
Loneliness thrummed in the iron my mother reasoned

Would make me look good,
"Pressing," while she hummed over the rude

Sound the smell of the board embodied.
I stood near her, holding the wood I toted

For the Home Comfort Range. What virtues
Remain to keep the muses from squirting

Drops to dampen my state as I come
Around to represent my home

While cruising on *The Good Ship Laureate*.
How many times I have wanted to be a rhapsodist.

The scene outside my picture-window?
A housing-development without transcendental

Moods in any dough my mother kneaded.
My temperament leads me

To sing of threads of hay-bale wire

13

# COW MIRE SONGS

To keep embellishments rare and entire

For a song: if my dream-head's illusory,
My dreams deliver dreams, accessories

For the little pink pigs among the wisteria
As I swing alone near one hack-bush's hysteria

Every fall when I rise up into those ropes,
Propping my legs against a poplar, playing rope-a-dope

And eating the berries which look like beads on a black
string
And taste so good I might turn

Into a raccoon or possum, squirrel, rabbit.
I love Cow Mire as much as I love the habit

Of running away from funerals when someone dies.
I went to so many, my mother saying, "Want to see your
Aunt Vi,

She looks so good lying there in state."
I think to myself that all death's estate

Works against me – neither better nor worse,
With ends and arms, emotion's coarse

Tearing away without teaching me anything but grief,
My scars carrying me in duress too brief

For standby, since grimness seems reality,
A dodge for me; sets me free to dally.

Personal history's temperaments modify
Until I am free to rectify

# SHELBY STEPHENSON

The picture we bear one moment at a time
As another lead from slights of virtual incline.

# POSSUM OBLIGATORY

The grin is haunting.
Bullets collect in my father's hands.

The moon hangs a furry clout.
His trigger finger makes a meal for the table.

Heaven is somewhere else for the animal.
She carries twenty-two on her back.

Her spouse seems helpless in the persimmon.
His gaze and my father's are one.

The little ones scramble nearby.
The .22 cracks again,

"Hand me another bullet, Son."
Decades sweep a sling of blood.

## BIG RED

Ever sharp and fighting for victory
Limps across the Irving tract,

His feet altering matter
Daylight shimmers out of darkness.

Eyes enter prisms; pupils motion concerts.
Every print hunts character, fortifying

A company of hunters
Gathering around their trucks.

Across clearings, out of hearing,
I imagine Big Red in a den, green with will

To leap, how cool, a sanctuary,
At times, a trifle, emphases, silences.

# NORTH AMERICA'S ONLY NATIVE MARSUPIAL

The revelation of a pouch soothes humankind.
The babies snuggle like grubs and sniff

Like furry puppies to secure their nuzzles,
Eyes wide with clairvoyance.

Who started the cry that Opossum's ugly?
Her fifty teeth come always ready.

Too much contemplation induces a lack
Of respect for the peaceful elemental.

The true view is the practical other,
Once you see the little ones ride their mother's back.

## THE MULES

I climbed under the fence where they wallowed,
The lot-wire, barbed, connected.

My conversion seemed true as miracles,
A benefit my mind charged oracles.

Black got up first; like a prophet,
She spoke to me, her tail lofty

As a bucket of water I drew from the well,
The chain making my hands tell

What it's like to prefer Gray.
Distortion always works memory,

For Gray's the gentlest mare,
Her testament come down from where

To tease me because I am the man
For whom endurance myths more sources than

Refreshment stores in falling rain,
Truing my inability for revelation in a thing

Of consequence, the way
I follow Black and Gray like a play,

Spring, summer, fall; winter's timely
Catch-up for voice defines me.

The spectral I long for in their eyes,

# COW MIRE SONGS

A meteor of snow, pleasure without guise

From childhood's custom to charm
And command the soul from fields to barn.

# BANJO-HEAD

As noble one asks,
"Could he be a crook?"
Ten thousand martyrs
    Consume an undying con.

Does not kindness separate
Gullibility from the living picture?
Banjo-Head wreaks
    Ever to suffer any lecture.

To intimidate his brothers and sisters
He draws in an open breath
And lines up another way to bluster
    Liberty while Virtue sulks.

In his eyes Nature stretches
Out her arms to embrace him.
He lets her thoughts topple reaches
    For big bucks adorning a whim.

In unison with his schemes
He gets the pastures and roadsides
To grow up in weeds.
    The presence of a higher thing he derides.

Beyond the human, yet so,
He loves to taste fame,
Epitome of the throw
    Of his own voice; his ear, the same

When he was little

# COW MIRE SONGS

And hid five dollars in the chimney
Outside where he could settle
  For a ball-glove with the money.

  Where it came from, I can't say,
Appropriated for lives
As words work and fare
  To predict his future acts.

## THE MAN SEEKING WATER LETS THE WATER-WITCHER HOLD THE VINE

"I just hold this twig in air,
Out from me, like this, over immensity –
This Y-shaped rod in the whole world's door?
I call it doodle-bugging; it's my cup of tea.
I am a water-finding champion, the Bird
Of The Water-Witch – and I do not fail to be heard.

"Now a divining rod's my way: my wall
Is cluttered with what pseudo-science empties in lens
To make me look funny: well, my daughter Melissa is a jewel,
A real water-witch: she uses any piece of lumber
She finds, an L-shape, her favorite; she holds it in her hands:
And I have seen that stick wobble all around.

"It's got to be a gift from on high,
This vining-rod business, sort of like catching a musky through the ice,
Or taking a bear ice-fishing and kicking his main artery
To bring the warmth on in such a place,
Plus seeing the look on my daughter's face when none
Other than a red-faced boy shows up with a mouthful of
worms as solution.

"Son, I say, What's happening to you?
            You know what he says? *Mister, like I say: you've
            got to keep your worms warm.*
Oh how me and Melissa make water-witching new

23

# COW MIRE SONGS

As that so the ground yonder might prompt
People to gather and heave sighs for the Word.
We court creation in a fallen world."

So, I watched Charles; that was his name. He stood
With his daughter, as if Nature was all
Enraptured with just themselves, bone and blood
Crawling in their bodies to make the twig a self.
I said to myself: what foolery: still
I could not explain the ritual of the father and child
Doing this hand-number with a vine and making it talk,
The standers there rubbing their chins and frowningly
Subconsciously shuffling their shoes in the sand in quick
Respites harkening back to the first baby's cry,
A mess of senses focusing in the dark,
Awkward worlds, shuddering, fallen.

## STORMS

This hill has howled and blown around all night.
I think of the word "cyclone" my father
Would use, a bad cloud coming up. I count
The seconds he'd tell when Robert Johnson

*Got blowed in scuppernong vines way yonder*
*When we lived in the plankhouse and Maytle*
*And me got married, before you were born,*
*And we built this nice brick for your mammy.*

To live life! Every time I think the wind
Might come up and I can push some Spirit
In this pen to pose a tug of words thin
Though they seem, I receive and inherit

Him, his checkerboard, while pines gather ice
In rows the Long-leaf marks on Sanders Road.
Show perseverance, I say to myself.
We know how freedom can be, though a load,

Good one for him. *This house is safe, my son,*
*But you could throw a possum through the walls*
*Of the plankhouse.* How essential to sane
Ideals writing the things which mark the fall,

Alone, as I am now, my family
Existing in chances wind might howl – dogs
The foxhounds my father kept to pursue
The red or gray, Novembers, Finch's Bog.

# GUNS

Suddenly he pulled a rabbit out of his hair – *hurrah*
In a hunt shot full of Thanksgiving ritual,
A gun going off in a hedge
A ways away, not out of hearing,
The number-8 shot scattering air –
He unbridged his 12-gauge, full choke Iver Johnson.
The shooter welled up the trouble his eyes
Teared up into a baby-bunting in a drawer-chest,

The whole stance of being one hunter stopping
To receive autumn's falling changes
Natural as a step toward the road running
Away from the rabbits, real men loafing
Amid sacrifices surfacing hunting season
To let the cottontail live and be itself
And come back to its squat near the ridged furrows

Where the boy would not go again with gun aflame.
He put his single-barrel in a corner, a circle of sun wide
As the picture window of the company-bedroom.
In his mind he could hear pops in a hedge
Forever golden for November, the boy
There, his hair bloodying alarm for peace to crack the air.

# THE SHORT WOMAN OF PAUL'S HILL

Thelma Allen's legs curl on the rungs of her chair. Her
plumpness suits her red-face, round as a moon cycling
her common marriage to Roof Allen. She knows people on
this hill refer

to him as "Castrate Man." Every small farmer contacts
Roof to cut the smelling blood with his razor to empt a
boar's balls down in grasses of hog-squeals, red eyes,
and rot-gut

whiskey. Thelma does not rise from her chair to see the
spillage one pig's life grooms for the table. She smoothes
her apron and keeps crocheting a work-sock baring a
monkey's

face with tears. She lives to serve company coming, her
husband, her garden, and me. Soon she and Roof will
leave my father's Place to be tenants somewhere else.
Forever she's

perched in her chair like a wren fluttering looks away, as if
hums point out to me devotions I shall never know in this
world, yet take for granted that Fate shall be inadequate to
glow

her chair, needle, and sock for Destiny to find a lock and
undo it for lessons I cannot mock, an operative probable
as Thelma Allen's storms ever hard-handing men and
animals.

# COW MIRE

This morning, chill March charges the sun's
Name bright as bronze glowing on the plankhouse.
I walk through it again and feel uplifted,
Transformed in truth's beholding to guts

Spinning in God's laundry, a wash out
Of intestines, autumn's leaves, old age, women,
Their wrinkles swallowed up in streams of Cow Mire's
Ferns, hickory, haw, poplar, ash.

I am not surprised at all. My mood's a guest
To bugs, goose-grass, masterpieces,
*The Devil's Cookbook*, that stake Great-grandpa Manly

Drove in the corner around 1900, after he walked home
From Jamestown, the Civil War growing
His eighteen brothers and sisters, his father,
Our Pap George (died 1886) selling July,
Price tag, $413.25, into more property
Than human chattel should shelter in 1851, a calculable
Bursting of mistakes in history's bosom of sales
On this hill: so now you know.

         One more line
Let's advance: call up the deer,
Dogs, hogs, the talents and characters of fiddlers,
Banjoists, guitar players, singers,
Out of impression's events July must have known,
Her title, "House Servant," listed in co-habitation records.
The difference between a butterfly and a turtle is that
The Holy Ghost gets too much wind in those days people

28

# SHELBY STEPHENSON

Were considered property: how does one grow old
And know nothing but abandonment,
Zero about how to stay young and aspire
To beauty and be new as July's name.

I experiment on endless seeking.
Cow Mire: named for the cows that sank
Up to their souls to find stability,
No pause or preservation; germinate,
Renew seasons, remain sensible.

## ANNIVERSARY SONG

Lightning bugs dance on the grass there
To sighs of lovers;
They kiss wet lips dry, hug
Through dresses and trousers,

Saying goodnight under light's
Dark as unmanageable lives
Keeping worlds, making time,
You, checking into other schools

And teaching delight to children,
While life turns me from law,
To our families, merging now,
Your face, mine, love, one.

# RACCOON SUNNING

A hunter grows in this place
Between rings on the tail
And sleep turning sun to flowers.

November bleeds blankness.
A dog slobbers in its waking.
A cat meows extended scowls.

The hunter's son murmurs
To think anyone could kill a thing so pretty.
Finale descends without grace.

Bumble bees thrum fear.
In the jacket, the tail hangs from one shot-bag.
A briar's hapless as a song.

# THE MULE GRAY

A shoulder-push in and up and I
Could get the rollers to roll on the track,
My basket full of corn shucked for her trough
In the corner of darkness and musk:
A toss of her neck's pure Mule,
          A grayness in whiteness with flecks
And stars, her warm sides pulsing
Aromas of corn-weevils and manure-mush,
Reeking memory's sanctuary, a primitive church,
Mules, tied to limbs, swishing flies.
Gray knows I hold her eye to eye –
Her forehead like masonry, the strong neck-ripples,
Gentle Gray, standing at her corn
To swing without muzzle or reins,
No work, just play in a steady jar of looks
For me to learn that we must die.
I was eight and woke Mortality up one morning,
          A geography of place chaos presents
In retrospect through the nostrils of this mule.
I learned Gray might end up as glue,
Just one old mule's momentum,
Something a child might paste in a memory-book,
Though I cannot say for sure what happened to her.
I must have been at school in a dream,
My head in languages to understand dying
Without hysteria or passion for art,
Gentle Gray, force, a tone of gravity and twinkles,
Gifts to me, her companion, loving her ears pricked
Forward in the steadying furrows
We walked at her pace, not mine,
Until limitations necessarily imposed

# SHELBY STEPHENSON

And I woke up one morning and she was gone
   Without me anymore.

# THE FIRST SOLDIER

I ever saw was Charles Ray Barbour.
When he stepped on the bottom plank
Of the house I was born in
I heard the board creak and the nail holes
Let go the nails my father whomped.
He certainly was not a carpenter.

Charles Ray worked the fields around.
Once he hit with his hammer an electric fence conductor,
You know, one of those little white
Porcelain spools farmers wrap
Their fence-wire on to keep the hogs in?
That's what I mean: I never asked him
About the war, what Korea was like,
How he kept it out of his mind.

He got a piece of the porcelain in his eye,
Married June, his distant cousin. They moved in with his
Parents, Mr. Johnny and Miss Bessie.
Honeymooners did that in the country in the fifties.
Families were families back then.
Charles Ray wore glasses as long as I remember.

# MARCH

The month of the windy hill, after the ice storm
Knocks out power and leaves me with hope
My cell might keep ringing for normalcy
While the full moon wreathes its orange.

Jupiter stays near as seeing for good the sky
If we could, infinitesimally we.
Cricket needs grooming for the weather
Warming the days blowing by the trees.

March: go out to the Scag and start it,
Mow the meadow with grace for green,
For the purple martins, too, I first saw
On the 22nd, a male scout, and a female.

The sheer weight of fits and starts
Saves me from sameness, gives a mysterious
Liveliness to itches, yodeling, memory.
Black and Gray want to pull the plows.

I want to see Percy at the door again.
"Do you have some weeds I can sling?"
Ah! The question comes before lawns,
When the yard on Paul's Hill is naked.

Go get the slingblade, I say,
And cut the ironweeds. He shuffles off
Like someone seeking nonchalance and gayety,
Someone silent, small, and singular of all things.

The Scag stays ready; I must be careful.

# COW MIRE SONGS

The hillside is steep and slides in the ditch;
Makes a burden which shifts out over my worries
That I shall not take chances when mowing.

I shall not offend the last dandelion.
Leave it for the dream repetitive universes know,
For the fact of imagination and eternity
The truth of things stays low for, like a hog.

Tubers turn to worms for Middle Creek.
The sand lapping the bank is white.
It is good in the right place,
As bad is good in the wrong place.

The time longs for rides on donkeys, a palm
Sunday and a Good Friday.
Christianity takes a long time.
The supreme month marks March when God is busy.

# AN EEL

Now you take an eel?
Under water all the time, soft-finned,
  Resembles snakes, broad-nosed or sharp.
  I love the freshwater eel, caught many
  In Middle Creek, wholesome when fried.

  Tastes better than a flogging strap.
Gets mixed in the line like a dancer on an aerial rope
  At the circus, always turning and twisting.
  No wonder grass-like weeds may be eel-grass.
  Eel beds are like bivouacs you can slide into
yourself.

  A brood of young eels will nibble
Caught minnows on a string.
  Water-snakes will do that too.
  I have never speared an eel with an eel-spear.
  I imagine that's a pronged instrument for a pond
especially stocked.

  I know some eely people, eel-like, eerie,
Some dressed in eel-skin.
  On a bar stool in a tavern you might see a woman
  In a tight-fitting dress.
  Sounds like a line in a Whispering Bill Anderson
  song.

  My mother could solid fry eel.
She'd cut one up in little links and drop them
  In a paper sack with proper amounts of flour and
salt and pepper.

# COW MIRE SONGS

You talk about something good! I feel my wits
happily eaten.
You can't beat that kind of eating.

Eels are slimy as pure form.
I want to say, "Pardon me. Hello Worm."
And then I undo my haste and eat the browned eel
Full with free effect.
To dream of eels is to never wonder whether
language might die.

Much of poetry is like eels.
There are so many in the loose grass in the water
Of logs and limbs in Middle Creek.
You cannot defile them.
They swallow the hook as if they're trained.

Contemporarily, I feel like the lost child
Who will never fish in the creek again
For the eel, let alone the robin redbreast or the gar,
The horny-head or the horse-fish.
The eel is like a dog or cat in a company of otters.

Sometimes I think the eel's got oil on its body
Which water creates until the substance
Re-enters the slime which becomes
The overrated, civil paraphernalia
Of fishing a stream which shivers like the world's
spine.

# APRIL PASTORAL

Now is the field sunned bright
Round the bluebird's nesting heart.
The four eggs pale, as if shined pewter
Becomes a radiance of duty
When I lift the lid to see
What the three buzzards circling must feel,
An accurate instinct the martins seize
In their return to promote this frieze.

# CHANNEL CAT

Fish, a foot long, tail
Forked, that dot a sign:
Horn, *will work alone to hurt*
*Instinct no bar to boy with pole.*

He's daydreaming on the bank,
His shadow a most elemental thing
More than his room at home
A strike might prove no brain.

More than skin allows the hands
He worries about the size of something
To annoy the threshing out of the marsh
The train-whistle never tells him more.

What aura the fins experience,
The lightest finger on the line,
Lead-line of fairest less or more
Than one fisherman might stand.

Quietude's an elucidation of detail:
One long flail of bones, needle-sharp,
Deep inside something a good deal more
Than gills (must grab them behind).

If it bites it swallows bait and hook.
A towel won't work to uplift the headline:
*Boy cannot use tweezers or pliers.*
All hands and eyes, he stays faithful.

To create, he says, living is possible.

# SHELBY STEPHENSON

The table's set without modifications.
In his heart the channel makes its bed.
The boy sees flicks of the invisible,

Even as he cuts his cat behind the gills
So that he can pull the skin toward the tail,
Down with the pliers the way a sock
Tends to slide away from the heel.

The head he tosses into the hedge.
Catastrophe purrs and dances with bees
For a mouth full of whiskers and eyes
Glazed with nature's gifts in progress.

## BLISTERED

Words! Get on, involved in particulars!
*Throw that pallet down in the sand and wait!*

Enjoyment's identity burns pigment.
The girls pass me by for long sleeves, a cap.

Watch the red fox and possum prance and shine,
Unselfconscious as I would like to be.

Learning's variation becomes some rules.
Words may be true as very rotten wood.

There may be deep streams in your complexion.
There may be light darkness, like poetry.

Frightening, to be in the sun too long,
Fair-skinned, red haired, freckle-faced, pearly brown.

Without a lesson-plan, go for the pier.
Lie down under it: hard at seventeen.

Body hard, muscles swelling – jumping round,
The Charles Atlas course, come-on, one mag ad.

Hype charges on before us, though I am
The one blistering in the hot, beach sun.

Two books in the plankhouse I was born in,
*Sears Catalogue* and the *Holy Bible.*

Peeled skin is the life of apprenticeship.

# LIBBY CAMPBELL

Libby Campbell's a wonderland
In and of herself, her tutelage
Bringing currents warm to Cool Spring Elementary
Because she believes in helping
Young people, third-graders, especially.

County Iredell's vibrant with words
And promise when Libby promotes and
Manages the hunger every soul finds in
Poetry: consider her love of children.
Behold, she volunteers to help them
Easily as she creates an atmosphere,
Leading them to orchestrate their writings for assisted-
living residents,
Letting them appreciate the need to remember and create.

# POSSUM TO THE FLEAS

The dulled death I faked
Even as the automobile sacked
My babes clinging to my back.
Then I survived my rescuer

Who stopped in the road to pick
Me up on her way down to the Vet,
The Volvo's space in that cargo
A claustrophobia of rubbish.

I inhaled the rubber in the tire
Spare in its hovel; the battery-charger's
Acid in my nostrils, too,
And an avocado which escaped

A Food Lion plastic bag.
The worst, though, was to lose that joy,
Memorable as song-like poems
I crooned on my way to the moon.

Virginity crawled on into the usual.
When you fleas ascended as she
Lifted the lid, I expired in a whoosh,
My last wish – remember my name: Marsupial.

# A STORY OF THE STARS

A microphone is staticky

On the stage. Holding its crackles,
Adorning the crowd's breath,
It does not pretend to need a voice.
Even its stink is smelly,
Vented with spittle from previous stars.

It owes no space either to George D. Hay,
WSM (We Shield Millions) or a winter's reckoning.
At the Ryman, Lew Childre slackly
Taps in his patent-leather shoes.
Similarly, it sends shouts home to his Alabam!

It does not prance for fame.
The tuning people in the audience crave
Planets in a landscape of tourists.
It expects to finish each concert with ease.
Being a fan of Bill Monroe, this sound box

Squeals at times under tweaks of breath,
Especially in the spring,
When the wind – the breaths of stars
Any known dreamer longs to bring
Out of memory – quietens in a corner,

With makers of the masks with those special mouth
openings.

# MAMA'S WORDS

One time Mama was watching the "News with Dan
Rather"
and he said something about puberty and Mama
turned to me and said, "Son, what did he say?" I said,
"Puberty, Mama, you know that word?"

"No," she said, "I know Poverty. I did have a little wagon. It
was red.
We had a little goat and it was my horse."
She was standing at the sink in the kitchen. I was
about forty. She started talking about her father.

She said she was six, waiting to walk to school
when her mother, name was Auriba, told Orron
to go to the hog parlor to check on his father
who went to feed the hogs. And she said her brother

Orron was twelve and he came running back to the house
down there in Elevation: it was forty-three days
after my family moved from around Newton Grove,
she said: Orron was crying, whining how his daddy was

dangling by a rope in a tree, a mulberry tree, she said.
I had never heard that story. The singing began
soon after. She started humming "Amazing Grace."
I never knew my grandmother Orby (no one could

pronounce the name *Auriba*.) She died before I
came along in 1938. I think we
did have a happy life, didn't know any
better: my mother was one of nine children, two

dying in infancy of cholera (Charlie Emanuel and Parley
Nathaniel).
You pick up what feathery song
in the air and go on. Grandmother Orby raised all the
children,
never remarried. My mother married my father

when she was sixteen and he was twenty-one. They were
married for fifty-eight years. My life was like a
rose in a cleft, snug and surrounded by moss along
ditches.
Forever seemed available, flowing

flavoring right up to waking up with
character and some clarity this morning:
the hymn in the hum resides. My mother drifts
away in the shallows. I believe in the single fact

that happiness happens when first love appears
under the stars and purpose takes care of living
with ruling that motion's boredom
which will not sit still for long.

The world does not dissolve. It gets along
on its own until our hearts patter for Fear
to take a seat beside the little animals -- the chipmunks,
squirrels, owls -- until we see a line before ending

takes place and there is no other, the unknown
diving like the squirrel I saw this morning
sprint across the backyard, a universal
jump right where formation takes place

and we can stand up among our family
members and remember the good within
what seems a dead drop to the ground

# COW MIRE SONGS

once someone cuts the rope from the limb.

# OCTOBER LOVE

I awake in mourning
for sassafras so true
the redbird seems calm
under the feeder. The lawn

browns to call more burning
so that I might see you
without detail of squirm
and rush to get shopping done,

to celebrate, without mourning,
that we may survive the true
shades our love shapes in calm
resorts to red the lawn

expanding with leaves burning
autumn's come-on for you
as I do without the squirm
summer's worms have done.

## BAG WORMS

Amazing: I don't know much
About them. I see them in such
Splendor, early June, their nests
Cozily-limbed as if to test

My tolerance. I turn my back
And go back in the house to sack
The garbage, my mind lost
In reverie of what's

To come. By mid-August I learn.
The larva's wrapped silk in lean
Leaves and twigs as if
To broadcast some special riff

I don't hear happening
Outside my stoop, a thing
I take for granted without acceptance,
My eyes and head set by chance

I might wake to sleep no more
With insects fuzzy at my door.
I'm amazed at their appetite.
They host foliage I don't even suspect.

# PANTOUM FOR OLIVER

When I think of Oliver, I think of Listerine,
A mouth void of any stink which might last
Through the trials he put us through – yikes!
For there was always more.

A mouth void of any stink which might last
The usual flop-down-anywhere basset,
For there was always more
For a dog that wanted to be king.

The usual flop-down-anywhere basset
Was not what to expect from Oliver's ramifications
For a dog that wanted to be king.
A dog-trainer who needed lithium

Was not what to expect from Oliver's ramifications.
He wanted to be leader of the pack and that is why,
Yes, a dog-trainer who needed lithium
Recommended a choke-chain for Oliver, outright.

He wanted to be leader of the pack and that is why
I gave him to the Moore County Hounds: the trainer was
not lying.
Recommended a choke-chain for Oliver, outright,
As he was not the image of some picture-perfect Rover.

I gave him to the Moore County Hounds: the trainer was
not lying!
Some blunt responses those hounds moiled to rave
As he was not the image of some picture-perfect Rover,
For the rabbit-hunters wanted devotion.

# COW MIRE SONGS

Some blunt responses those hounds moiled to rave:
When I think of Oliver, I think of Listerine,
For the rabbit-hunters wanted devotion
Through the trials he put us through – yikes!

# THE TERRITORIAL BASSET

I told the vet Oliver was pushy,
that he would nip at my mother's heels
as she walked past him on his L.L. Bean
bag in the corner of the room, a feel,
my mother said, like stepping on a cone
a long-leaf pine dropped on a snake-like bone.

Dr. Neal winced, adjusted his spectacles:
"I have three Pembroke Welsh Corgis and when
I walk them by a certain stout lady
on my block all three at once smell her thin
ankles and she, of course, is real startled
to sense the sound of teeth through her stockings."

I looked at Nin as if my eyes were rocks.
She knew we made a mistake by being
in those stuffy chairs. I felt like a horned lark
lost from its mate, alone in sun shining
in wayward wind with only a sunset
near to lower color to horizon;

yet I knew I had to thank him: he looked
out the window of his veterinary
there along Midland Road, Southern Pines: "Look,"
he said, "it's funny that a basset scares
anyone, for slower than molasses
they are in driveways and roads for passing

cars to screech and blow horns and halt to keep
from running over them like rugs." I rose
from my seat, took Nin's hand in mine, as if

to say, We all need a good, solid dose
of bourbon or moonshine to quell the faint
light which comes under our shuffling feet.

# LAUREATES AND CRICKET START OUT AT RED ROOF PLUS +

*for Anne Russell*

If Cricket won't a dog like Sam, Harry Crews's Sam,
She would talk and make history right here in Manassas,
An ill-thought-out happening now, since Crick and I
checked in to the Red Roof Plus +,
The TV on, the weather-woman "breaking down the
weather for Everybody."
Cricket does not care: she was fifteen on June 22, 2017,
kind of old,
But not uncommon for a Norwich Terrier. She's nearly
blind,

Her instinct's like a twelve-point crow's foot or quail-flush
in a blind.
She's curled on the rug now at the door. I imagine Crews
walking Sam
Outside in the gray and falling drizzle, the October foliage
a Plus + old
Made new before my eyes? As Richard Hood would say
to every person in Manassas,
"You kidding me?" I think the laureates are driving in the
rain, Everybody,
To get to a luncheon at noon in Merchant Hall of Hylton
Center, a far cry from Plus +.

I am lost for words, Anne: out from Wilmington floats Plus
+
Over a dune at Carolina Beach, raising a blind

# COW MIRE SONGS

Which feels like a dream to me and to Everybody
Who shuffles toes in sand for Sam.
He has walked there, too, I'll bet, far from this landscape
around Manassas
Which spreads into Miracle Mile Shopping Centers and
battlefields of old.

Soon I shall join some old
Friends a few miles from Red Roof Plus +.
The event is called "In the Company of Laureates."
Manassas
Will feel like five states shaking for poetry: blind
Beauty truth shall spin to Silence. Sam
Will appear with Harry Crews on a fishing bank for
Everybody.

The darkness shall lift and Everybody
Will burp without making any sound, as if old
Farts come to hold unremembered dogs like Sam
In their lives again. I shall salute Cricket, Plus +,
Give her a hug right under the hanging blind
Where she sleeps on the rug in the Red Roof Plus + in
Manassas.

I will say under my breath, "Manassas,
I love you," to unison the whole countryside. Everybody
Will rise up from their chairs, as if blind,
And say their poems in lyrics and images of old
Men and women made little children again, Plus +,
And Crews will say to Sam

Once more in Manassas: "Sam, you, my dog of old,
If you won't a dog Everybody knows you would bark Plus
+."
And The Poet would rise from behind a blind and say *We
love you, Sam.*

## OCTOBER BIRDS

It could be the fields sport food;
it could be the fall doing what it should.
It could be the score of the pileated;
it could be the seasons satiated.
It could be the birthday month for Mom and Dad.
It could be a mystery more good than bad.

The birds call me to clean out their houses.
This morning I emptied a nest: thousands
of strands, straw, the bluebird spurned
because two red-shouldered hawks returned,
circling and landing at the round door
of the Bluebird Unlimited box for more

shrieking plaintively a tall *kee-ahh*,
repeating with lifts of their banded tails,
heads down in grass, too close for the brilliant
blue of the male Eastern Bluebird a zillion
humans would love to sing and portray,
let alone wear that tinged blue of one egg, female.

## THE THREE-QUARTER-TON FORD PICKUP TRUCK, PLUS A 1949 FORD COUPE

Boy, Shub, will you never forget foxhunts
and the short trips to church in that black truck,
the five of us (sister Rose had moved out).
The naugahyde smelled up the morning sun.

That truck was car, farm-rig, foxhound kennel.
Mom did not drive it. She'd wait for Pea-green,
The Ford coupe Dad bought. Shub was eleven.
Mom drove it round and round a pecan tree.

That is how she learned to drive. She was short,
five-foot-two, she said, just like the song sort
of sings; so she sat on a tall pillow:
reached the pedals. Age: forty-four, willow,
Mom who made cakes for sale at Curb Market
to send me to school; she was good-hearted.

# DID HANK DO IT THIS WAY?

Or did Luke the Drifter – and God write them,
The Drifter of The Drifting Cowboys Band,
Of broken hearts and too many parties,
Dreams of mama, funerals, shiny cars.
His talent was hailed by all who heard him.

I grew up singing Hank's songs and sad hymns.
Psalms and recitations I heard as poems.
The poetry in them gave my heart ease –
Or did Luke the Drifter?

"Be Careful of Stones That You Throw," wrung from
The pen of "Little Blossom," made Bonnie
Modena Dodd wave. She played steel guitar
With Tex Ritter in the 1940s.
Or did Luke the Drifter?

## SESTINA

October fog surrounds Paul's Hill.
Paul S R is dead except in the mind.
Paul Junior is dead, too, though you may see
him in center on the old Cleveland ball-field,
his father, this Paul S R, as he called himself,
wearing his Stetson along the third-base line.

Paul Junior comes to bat, draws a line
in the sand at the plate: he awakens Paul's Hill
with a double to right, he, himself,
in his father's eyes, a guide for his old man's mind.
*That's my boy*, says he. The ball-field
draws smoke from Paul S R's cigar; the fans yell to see.

That's a sample of what the father and son see.
Baseball, in fact, becomes Paul Junior's line
to Louisburg College. The ball-field
could have been at Cleveland on Paul's Hill,
except for one extra Paul Junior's mind
takes on at his coach's advice, though Paul, himself,

is not comfortable. He wants to be himself
when a fly-ball comes to him in center: see
him, if you will, making his glove a basket his mind
shapes as the ball misses the glove and makes a line
for Paul's chest where the ball strikes: Paul's Hill
fans go dizzy with oohs and ahhs washing the ball-field.

When he comes home he smells like a ball-field.
Thread-marks shine on his chest; he, himself
seems eager to stay on Paul's Hill

and farm, hitch up the mules, Black and Gray, see
them pull the McCormick wagon in a steady line
to the cornfield to get up corn and settle his mind.

Paul Junior does not become Paul S R's mind,
though both follow local games around any ball-field.
Paul S R never forgets that refrain, his line –
*That's my boy* – every time the son himself
makes a good catch or lays down a bunt to see
how fast he can leg it out toward first base on Paul's Hill.


*That's my boy*, the mind of Paul Junior, himself,
and Paul S R , One, as long as a ball-field readies fans to see
what a line draws to help keep baseball alive on Paul's Hill.

# SONG OF THE HONKY TONK

We're almost persuaded
To swab ourselves in pain.
Your lips moisten and run.
Mine stay open in vain.

The fiddle slurps the strand.
Your hair catches the wind.
The Lone Star Ballroom swells
Waltzes, foxtrots, refrains:

"I Can't Stop Loving You,"
"Rambling Man," "Lost Highway,"
"I Can't Help It," of course,
Plus, "Hello, Mary Lou."

What does holding come to?
The wind, path from Adam
To Eve, Kitty Wells, Job.
Down-lane spells log-cabin.

"Darling, I Could Never
Be Ashamed of You!" My
Mind wanders the way home
To your pretty face, smile.

In "Almost Persuaded"
Your ruby red lips seal
More unrequited love
Than hurts in our embrace.

## COUNTRY GIRL

I will tell you this, my own country girl:
You may shake like a bee-buzz in a tree,
Dance on a DJ's CD in a twirl,
Use your tip-toes to set the drum-roll free.
You may ripple like my Middle Creek flows;
Yet, if I ask you to speak for yourself,
I doubt if you'd say, "Give me a Bud, Shub,
I'll show you how to guzzle myself
Off this barstool right here at the Draft House."
I'm just a country boy, money have I none.
Stars be stars no sun turns to golden souse
Any more than infinity's blue moon
Rises in the east to give me your face
The clouds and stars, my love, cannot erase.

## ODE TO OCTOBER

The birthdays of my mother and father:
They are gone from this world, though their motions
Make a pattern which quilts Rose, the daughter,

Gone, too, in fall's leaves dropping devotion
To colors and sails across the backyard
On Paul's Hill where you lived with precision.

Love weathers the cold, turns the hogs to lard.
I hear you say, "We must live off the land."
You did for fifty-eight years. A good bard

Might write your story, even form a band
To sing songs of love and hymns the gospels
Roll, soak, and scroll in Jordan River's span.

Everywhere I turn I see your models.
In my heart, year-round, October prospers.

# AUNT LINEY'S FUNERAL

And Mama said: "Son, would you like to see
Your aunt Liney lying in her casket?
She looks good, like she's dressed in her housecoat,
So warm and cozy, lying like a tree
Just fallen, still, with plenty of green buds,
As if she might rise, say Hello Heaven,
Goodbye, world, I will see you, my children
In the sweet bye and bye. You are my shrubs."

And Shub said: "Mama, I'd like to see her
As I saw her last; she said to me, lord,
Decades ago: Please come to see me, I
Won't be here long." Oh, how Mercy, I score
My pitch, awkwardly, saying my goodbye
In a way I cannot find the right chord.

# LETTERS TO FRED CHAPPELL

1

PRESENCES

I might come closer to saying who is
Speaking if I come right out and say I'm
The one, of course, in the wind who seizes
The ear, eye and tongue wadded in the mouth.

    Moving among the known and unknown,

We shift as the music settles the words
In Haywood County or Johnston or where
Any place vanishes to let birds course
Our beings with actual poise and freight,
Ways we let the melody hold the words.

    Heaviness is a bother too.

To use a pseudonym might only add
A seeming freedom; after all, a prop,
Like an itch, could disregard cures for bad
Lines, if there is clamor for one teardrop.

2

ON THE OTHER HAND

Is there a golden band, a goose of sorts
with feathers flying loose for boys and girls
who circle flag-poles in free-wheeling gyres
bumping and swaying over places warts
of artificers scrib and craft resorts
they build to shoot the moon to see in curls

and pantaloons a field for sport-stories?

And so I knew the boy way back I was,
this red-on-the-head Smoke, Shub, Shelb, Shel, Sheb –
pronounce the syllables where I grew up.
Who needs more? I will never know. Applause
For any wit still leaves Emily dead.
Who knew that Longfellow might play backup.

3

DEAR FRED

I was at Campbell when *River* came out.
I read the whole thing to my class: I'd shout

The Virgil Campbell figures when he shot
The Pigeon – "Sweet Jesus Christamighty Gawd,"

I'd fake a spit and swig and shout some more.
After class one boy came up, jarred the floor.

"Oh man, Did he really – say that?" Stallage.
"Yeah." The Baptists running the college

To this day hear Old man Campbell in their sleep,
"Somebody by God ought – "
 the flood still sweeps.

# TRYING TO GET TO THE BOTTOM OF IT

I try not to forget those days at home,
Though I would not like to live them again,
Alone with the chores and a currycomb
I used to groom Gray among the chickens
That ran out in the barnyard and mule-lot,
For telling you these details, I'm afraid,
Only makes any point I sharpen rot
Before it's ripe or, on arrival, dead.

Reveries under the shed's overhang
Close in on truths unbeholden to me,
Scrunched against the wall, sun sweet as sea tang,
The dew, too, dripping from the tin a spree
I cannot sing except to say it's so.
Childhood, the goose-pimples, moments of bliss
I sense from decades back, gains my long row
I keep on hoeing while I reminisce.

It all comes to not-knowing who I am.
I can smell a good promise now, and then
I am back for sure where I started from,
This Century Farm on Paul's Hill, the wren
Across the road, its song loud and clear, slaves
In their mounds of clay unmarked near Pap's stone.
Let me say again he's there among graves.
Is there an unknown definite in bones?

They could be dug up to show July's name,
In her homemade casket, though we must go
To Johnston County's courthouse for a claim,
That Bill of Sale that a certain "Negro"

# SHELBY STEPHENSON

Girl Pap sold for a few hundred dollars.
Enough. Our history's those documents.
I walk out by the garden of collards
My mother set out near the past's results.

I was a hillbilly when it was cool.
Far inside the culture I worked to play,
Sing songs I heard on radio; at school
I was asked to sing some songs I no way
Cared about: "They Were Doing the Mambo."
Recall the line: "While I just stood around."
That's how my life has gone, a patio's
Sure not cotton fields. Am I too far gone?

I saw Elvis in 1954,
Memorial Auditorium in
Raleigh, tail-end of Ferlin Husky Show.
The seats clank right now in memoriam
For Presley and Husky: Ferlin was star
After Hank Williams's death. I can draw
Elvis's mouth to the mike; his guitar
Is wearing something like a baby's throw.

*I got a woman way over town*
*That's good to me, oh yeah* – and the seats
Clatter the audience in one big drown.
He had just started recording with Sun
And Sam Phillips. RCA came shortly.
The rest is history: Faron Young said
No one could rent or buy a hillbilly
In Nashville: real country music was dead.

1956 I graduated
From Cleveland High School. I don't remember
Being serious: skipped: drank homebrew: made
Me closer to my father, Paul S R
And the wallop from his homemade whiskey.

# COW MIRE SONGS

We would turn out his thirty-five foxhounds
And their music prompted me to listen
To something inner, my own self alone.

I've told this many times before: he came
Into the company bedroom. I was
Filling out a long form. He called my name,
Two syllables he'd never said because,
I suppose, like most old-time southerners,
His talking sort of rolled out in a wad.
He flung himself down on the comforter:
I said, "Daddy, I'm going to college."

"Stay here with me and we will hunt and fish
And this place, Paul's Hill, will be yours someday."
Then he left me alone, echo, to wish
And wonder how I might work out the pay.
My sister-in-law left me at a dorm,
Lewis, in the lower quad of campus.
My Martin guitar I retired at home.
I am still getting used to that status.

If a frog had wings it would fly and not
Bump its rear-end across the ground to hop
Always into the unknown like the snot
Off a mule's nostrils or swampy runoff.
I'm saying childhood's Everything, almost,
The be-all in my life, I can tell you.
If I tried, I could not stand in as post
In some museum, tough as real lightwood.

I was not a sheep or goat: I had to
Face up to being alone, no money,
Except what I earned for daily meals, three,
Lenoir Dining Hall, morning shift. Mama
Made cakes she sold at Curb Market, Smithfield,
To help me get us through. That's love divine.

# SHELBY STEPHENSON

Ask me how I got through? I can't conceal
The way things happen to bring on sunshine.

I thumbed home first year: a janitor's job
At a radio-station in Smithfield,
WMPM: World's Most Progressive
Market: I soon learned the art of wheeling
Around in my chair: I worked the console.
I must have breathed acres of nicotine.
VU meter's needle my radio
Voice the bright red right level cleanly peaked.

Somehow I thought of Red Rooster Rudy
Out in the yard on Paul's Hill, my desire
For Frank Gallop waving my love for Trudy.
Bought a '54 Ford Victoria.
It had bad shocks. I want to tell all this.
Where could I go after the farm? Law School.
Oh oh oh. We failed each other, what bliss.
I turned that blessing to verse – overrule.

# SORT OF HOW IT WAS

*in memoriam: J. Dickson Phillips Jr. (1922-2017)*

I never brought myself to pray
      How I felt when he sat up
And looked me in the eye to say
      *I am not omniscient:*

*I think your talent's not the law.*
      As student I was spent.
I got a D in Agency,
      His class at UNC.

I was in my third year, Law School.
      I needed thirteen hours
To graduate. I never knew
      A rule I could follow,

Let alone do long division,
      Grade three: or Algebra
As freshman at Carolina.
      I flunked it, no hoopla.

Or say I did not know what I
      Wanted to do after
Ending up as English major.
      I worked as announcer.

I went to college unprepared.
      Looking backward I know
I always creamed subjects that mired
      To be me, make me go.

# SHELBY STEPHENSON

Of evidence, now memory:
     I was lost, my childhood
A flame of summer fields to be
     On fire come the autumn.

College seemed incidental. There
     I was, working my way
Through to let the days find me bare
     Of all but this plea: say

My intentions were good as gold.
     The clichés I did loath.
Even then, I was one grown, bold
     Little boy, twenty-four,

And still across from Mr. Phillips,
     I sat: he was a war
Hero, I learned, after his death,
     A paratrooper, Lord,

The Purple Heart, plus a scholar.
     Top of class, Davidson.
And so in 1963,
     My little beige Austin-

Healey Sprite I drove home and parked
     It among the ironweeds
In the backyard, our very large
     Place which smells *plantation.*

My roommate that year, Dick Olive,
     From Summit, New Jersey:
His friend, graduate of Woman's
     College, in Greensboro, pleased me.

She was teaching, Falls Church, outside

# COW MIRE SONGS

Of D. C. Dick got me
A date with friend Suzie Winter.
Her dad? A. T. & T.

That was March, 1963,
Same month Mr. Phillips
Said he did not know everything,
The same month my mother

And I packed my things good and well
At 314 West
University Drive, Chapel
Hill: renters: Boom Booms: test?

The Cannons were lovely people,
Y.Z. Cannon, barber,
East Franklin Street, Chapel Hill.
I don't know what "Y. Z." stands for.

After eighteen months with the firm
I took leave of absence.
I am still on leave, determined
To have fun in the arts.

They salvaged my life: if I had not met
Mr. Phillips, my teacher,
I might have been remaindered
Way out of touch and reach

Of my love affair with poems, words.
So I say a prayer
For Dickson Phillips, yards
To yell that He's my soothsayer.

To give my grief some perspective:
Grief's better than nothing.
That's a line from New Albany,

# SHELBY STEPHENSON

Mississippi: Faulkner.

Because grief's for my mother, how
        She wrote to Dean Brandis
On my behalf: I'm compelled now
        To tell the story: born

For poems and the arts to make
        Me over; left my Sprite
With my mother and bought myself
        $52.00 worth

Of books; enrolled as a student,
        University of
Pittsburgh. I knew the very first
        Night I would stay with books.

There were two in The Plankhouse on
        Paul's Hill: *Sears Catalogue*,
Southwestern Publishing's *Bible*,
        A shelf, one weighted log.

Lines on mortality stop me.
        I figure in my youth's daze.
A warehouse's long stash of trees
        Darkens folly, decay.

And it snows here and does not stop.
        Omniscience no one knows.
Thank you, Finiteness, for our lot:
        Yours, his, mine, the shadows.

# ELVIS

Thinking of words that would salvage him, wiggling
Before the microphone, 1954,
Raleigh Memorial Auditorium, my rolled-up sleeves,
Peg-legged pants a camel-turd brown – glory

Be rock-n-roll in the highest,
I was there, chauffeured by my brother Paul,
To see Ferlin Husky, the biggest
Name in country music after Hank, "That's all,"

He said, singing his final song, "I Feel Better All Over
More Than Anywhere Else."
The seats in the auditorium clanked in tunes
Fine, full, perfect as Paul and I
Scampered toward our car for the run

To Paul's Hill, Elvis's face already in the microphone,
"I got a woman, way cross town, she's good to me, yeah!"
Seat-bottoms went down like
The clatter of a train on a track piled with telephones.

"Here, here, here," he comes again,
His white suit shaking, guitar dressed
In something like a baby's bunting.
I was fifteen: I felt the blessed

Show I was witnessing, that haste of stardom
The close-up of fame becoming art,
The blast of records he made, bruising boredom,
With Sam Phillips at Sun, the center of the earth.

# SHELBY STEPHENSON

In a week or two Elvis Presley was on RCA.
The song, well, we know it, "Heartbreak Hotel,"
The ready throttle of his voice fully packed with grace,
With that extra salute to guts and secrets of nature.

I love to sing country music; yet I never sang
An Elvis song, for once he did it, it was done.
Impersonators come and go, dressed for flim-flam
And money to put in the bank and some for RCA and Sun.

And what's the matter? The Tupelo truck-driver's
Life drew all things in. Day became night.
Graceland became a tourist's quandary.
Elvis was gone mid-age. And his fans cried.

I don't know the part Colonel Parker played.
The personal Elvis became persona.
When sweet ducks puddled his way,
He could not appreciate the public's presence on his lawn.

# TO THE TICKS

Afflicted by heat hotter than a mink,
A he one from Pepper Patch this last day
Of June, the water off the shore something
I cannot word, so balmy, true, sun rays

Forgetting nature's call planned by doggie
Or a God that did not finish the job,
I brush air; a tick, looks like a poppy
Seed, sticks to my hand, looking for a home.

I'm alone. I need help, someone, rescue.
It's good I am in the bathroom: I flush
Him or her or it down the toilet's *whoosh*.
The sound craves boredom binges in a bush.
The creeps consume the water on my face.
To get the hell out of there, I itch, race.

# THE RINGING OF THE BELLS

*for the backyard bell collection, Coats estate & museum,*
*near McGee's Crossroads, NC*


Now I hear them—ding dong ding dong bell bell
above me, July 4th, church, firemen, school
bells out on Old Fairground Road, huge bells yond
flying back echoes of bells; maybe mine,
my Cleveland High School bell: Mr. Thompson times
the pull of his rope, oh, he's clonging now,
taking his pocket watch from his OshKosh.
Poe's, too, I hear them, "keeping time, time, time."
Mr. Tink collected bells; his 50's Cad
swanks the museum on the premises
along with farm-tools for one's benefit.

## SONNET FOR LIFE WITH ART

Art might say Beauty has been gone so long
Clamplitt shouts for Davison to take poems
I write about hogkillings on my farm.
Emily Dickinson! Tragic. "Failed poet,"
Buy his freedom. Go, Heaney, Hughes, Jarrell.
Ruth Ellen Kocher; oh my Keats, coming
for the Lowells; that's sure what time will tell.
Dear Melville? The obit misspelled his name.
Nash was real light, wasn't he? Oppen's stuff
Is political? Paz won't be the same.
Quarles: "Abused patience turns to fury." Must:
Rakosi, S. Sanchez, any Taylor,
Updike, Vaughan, Warren, Wright, Xin, Yeats, Zimmer.

# RENDEZVOUS

Your presence I design to hear
Everywhere, even Facebook's air
Or on the various foundations.
Your hug's worth a lake of stations
Our music plays on pitch and tunes,
Separation a cause creatures
Beauteous can be, you, the maid
With whom I wish to woo and stay,
      Goodness, emparadised.

Your eyes help your hands around me.
My surround no one sees, it's true,
For our charm disarms the civic
Work we do, dialogues, breathing
In and out to settle the spell
Growing outside never to dwell
On deception of our closeness.
You could be on islands off-coast.
      I could best sense as you.

The fish that swim in Middle Creek
My indulgences never seek.
I free reverie by default,
With real muddy boots my assaults
On our rapport with no despair,
For our strength we each shall wear
Like cover our first parents heard,
Expeditious while watching the birds
      As they feed little open beaks.

I am not a fool to love you.

# COW MIRE SONGS

I am your kind of man, as you
Said clearly so brave with spirit,
Austere, amending the outstripped
Praise seeing other goddesses
And gods before Heaven, the rest,
For now, we dream of every night,
Though separate, yet once again, all right
For all the world to see.

# INDEPENDENCE

You raggedy flag of July's minions,
Come higher from the dirt and let waving
Be holiday you salute with plenty
Of hats of straw and maids and men merry.
Let bells ring echoes over the cow-barn
At the Tink and Addie Coats Estate set
Aside this day for things windy and warm,
The Boy Scouts pulling ropes to raise their sweat
Upward the bells many timed tones downward
From full force to the hidden, yet still found
Once more on every summit and sound toward
The sky all the way, the stars, stripes around,
The twinkles rankling up unbottled heat
Nights fill with rockets showering
The Milky Way with swats
On the way to what heavens rise and bear
Fruit and, at last, support discord's absence,
When light shines on Dame Hymen's tight lips
To lap and lamp every Tuesday morn,
When I was a boy, before dreams took me
Asleep or awake and left me in bounteous
Recall of wrong numbers and poverty
And wilt in hills becoming mountainous,
Desire lounging big in weather's bounty,
Rules, too, searing how not to burn biscuits
Lovers miss while singing songs of sunshine.

Bring on the brainstorm, then, babe, and remove
The high chair for crowds to lean and pitch in
To tie a ribbon round the old oak, one
Of rainbow's hues for July, slave girl's few

# COW MIRE SONGS

Years as full person instead of three-fifths.
Let zippity spout without gagging
On popcorn and beer while boys play nifty
Stobs at horseshoes, one throw, success tilling
Real veins in a town hurting to be born,
Taken over by ones in time seeking
The school for shelter and some unforlorn
Adults on crutches imbibing as chiefs
Mark and swing inside their heads for the score.

## OCCUPATION: GRIEF

What old dump named Midden climbs many brief
Tosses by the familiar earth,
A basket of knives and dog bones named Grief.
We should daily live our lives to give birth
To flies that blow the slop and then render
It miraculously in heaps, I add,
Toward a sonnet a day for Susan,
And Tom, Kay and Nancy, Sally and Dad,
My troubling, trembling understanding *What*
As plastic flowers the wind resurrects
Without praising the rites I know as snot
Some farmer squeezes out of his life's wreck,
The death of his one mule, Mortality,
The far-off come-on to telegraphy.

## ONE MORE POEM

If you think I'm going
to make some sense here, bonging

and winging on the ropes
attached to the bells, rope-a-dope,

call it, just don't say so,
for I am tired of the hoe

and my row, too; Cricket's
way incomprehensible, a thicket's

worth of supper, breakfast, dinner.
I fight for her more; she's a winner.

On June 8, 2018,
she was seventeen: She's been

there and done that. We cannot
go back when Truth weighs in with knots

wadded up in balls of flab
and tethered to a Hairy on a bar

while it pecks
the suet in these letters

to what words word the light
and endure the jousts of drought.

# FIFTY YEARS PLUS

Nin
Is your
Nickname, palindromic Nin: it was

Long about 1963: I hear the window gasp
In a hush and your head thrusts out into
Nowhere but your red
Dress already coloring emotions of purest
Air I breathe, for you are Linda, my Buffalo gal,

Letchworth, your middle name (for your father's mom):
you
Ease into our years, expansive as the park itself,
The Letchworth family settling over there near
Cayuga Lake, though the closer one we
Hold dearer, as we courted there, and swam, and sailed: it
Was Owasco. I was working for American Telephone &
Telegraph,
Out of White Plains, as
Right of Way agent; bought land and easements,
The biggest part of two years, for micro-wave towers and
underground cables.
Handsome you are and undaunted still,

Wilson is your last name. In reality your
Interest is social service, the Wilson motto: "In Service to
Others Find Joy."
Lilting you off to live out of old romances, the name
Stephenson, too, fits us where we live today,
Out in the country where I was born in the plank house in
the hedge.

# COW MIRE SONGS

No one would ever say you are a southern belle though.

"Stephenson," you say, when anyone
Takes pleasure with your force and aim.
Easy as boredom, you reach for heights I know,
Purposeful, yet high on a mountain and way deep in a
valley where
Honeybees buzz waves of sounds,
Except the coming, gorgeous liveliness
No static can duplicate; I mean I say
Some real music comes out of your ukulele
On any given time; your harmony
No alternative offers except as we keep playing and
singing the old songs.

# MORNING SONG

Oh the fox led the dogs away from town
and praised them for their breath,
although he knew they could never catch
even a trace of his red self.

He was red as red in a flag on the fourth,
unlike the gray and he could level and lay
those hounds as if they were pups
chasing a tail on a string; no way

big red could give in to any dogs,
for he learned to evade from the possum,
North America's only native marsupial that could
hiss for mercy and roll over on his side somewhat

like the hunter's dream when Slobbermouth burned
that red's tail right into a hole or den
no hunter's horn could begin to miss.
No matter: less than a silhouette, so thin

That fox praised the sun's glare as a wall,
shadows only; no trace of fear
could trap inside a map of a wren's cap
to sing as loud an early song to any dog chasing one red's
rear.

# MANIFESTO FOR BEER DRINKERS

Don't drink many shots of alcohol.
You'll feel fuzzy; if you want to get drunk, try Wild Turkey.
Don't drive machinery: leave the Scag alone.
The mule stable's a parking place to tone
down your wish to be muscular and macho.
Think of the names of old dogs, for example, Hector.

He was Natty Bumppo's in the tales of Leatherstocking.
You might consider taking up boxing,
or, at least, the subject; consider Ali.
He needs no pardon; excuse me?
You're not so special to think anyone cares,
are you? Who you are or what you do gets lost among the
stars.

Stars make us feel infinitesimally small.
That is wonderful, don't you think? All
the ways to stare at the sky and count
your blessings instead of sheep.
Ba-ba-ba, Little Boy Blue, blow your horn
for the way deep south and for born-

again sects that hear sex is a way
to ring a bell or hit the clay,
especially when you want to steal home.
My advice is try the door-key or clone
your dog with Bullet to nose
out Roy's and Dale's sidekick Gabby Hayes.

Main thing is leave the brews in the store.
You will wake up more refreshed and more

satisfied with a mind that's stronger than tacks
by the passel or bushel; I don't hurt for backs
that sway or hair the wind blows
until you cannot stand to not close

yourself off to diversionary tactics.
Life's boring trail ends when you take a taxi,
instead of walking the several blocks,
if you are in NYC and your socks
work holes bigger than a drive might solve.
Have fun. Keep beer on ice. Then you will really rave.

# MY FATHER'S DYING

My mother dressed him in his pajamas.
He lay in the rented hospital bed.
I could see soak from his colon cancer.

The big room smelled like freshly rotting blood.
My mother's lips were humming "Amazing Grace."
Her presence, without words, made what she said.

White doves at the backdoor steps scratched and paced.
My father's eyes looked blue all the way through.
In openness they fluttered and stalled off base.

He was walking to see her, his one true
Love; he was twenty-one; she was sixteen.
"You two should get married," her mother mused.

The hospital scene: straight at the ceiling,
He stared, with love, "Don't you know I'm dying."

# GONE FISHING

I think I cleaned fish before I could walk.
I always knew how, seeing my father
go empt the guano sack full of bream
and bass and eel and pumpkinseed, catfish
(the channel and bullhead too) and so on:
the whistle dick, horse fish, carp, minnow, gar,
you name it, fish from our world, Middle Creek.
And we ate them, the littler, the better:
we fished to eat and ate to fish our catch.
I'd scale the little ones; then going up
with the knife at the tooter-hole, I'd pull
the entrails down through and into the gills,
saving every single bite not attached.
And little or big, I would always gap
the fish's hole with my sharp pocket knife
to reveal how I feel about bowels,
still wondering about the earth's rare place,
the seam and stream of eyes, of things global,
my mind losing presences in the found
comfort of measures sitting on burlap
on the bank of the creek, my lead line taut
for a bottom-feeder, my red bobber
a round and slight little boat in water,
my legs a dangle over the greenish
water where my string of growing fins fan
the fabric the water cleanses with ease
of slender waste and flourish of greater
practice without any new-healed passage
where the swell of fox or wolf I hear in
the distance, my walk out of the growth of
gravity and gravy, my mother at

93

our home sweeping the yard with her broom made
of dogwood (I must remember to cut
down a new one, as I hate to do, on
my way home) – a home in the face and hair
of wishing the fish would bite, for my walk
out to be more than a fisherman's luck,
a wet tail and a hungry gut, angel
over my shoulder not so ill as to tell
me I shall go home with a few boney
fish I shall see and smell in the popping
oil and pan, my mother frying the catch
for what it's worth without malice of age
or worry to follow through on matters
of fishing and not get caught up in it
to lose even a dram of scruple fish
always lugged sacredly as toes Jesus
keeps loafing as fish's great majesty,
plus the charm of hoping the world might bathe
downstream below the Rock Hole where Thread Tom
almost drowned me when I was a little
boy too young to fight the bad bullying
the bigger boys brag about, the fishes
themselves not hurting after the fishhook's
removed and they flitter their lives along
on a string and loiter while the water
snakes nibble to nudge into lethargy
free of hunger that the wild contention
a horse fish's head, lips, might really look
like Silver of Lone Ranger fame in a
stratagem to bow down now to say grace.

# THE LEANING BASKETBALL POLE

A squirrel-proof birdfeeder marks the pole
As hours keep passing the good spot along
To me tip-toeing my strolling to scold
The red-shouldered hawk in his singalong.

Decades have gone since Spug leaned his rifle
Against the barn: "I took the bullet out,"
He says, while bunching his height to stifle
The ball he shoots with a swish and a shout.

At dusk the barnyard's bulb hazes yellow
Enough to draw a gathering of old
And sporty boys; the neighborhood's dogs swell
The audience as Time holds me as its goal.

# EARTHBREATH

*for Carol Peters*

The earth's sweet-honeyed breath
flows summer, winter, fall, and spring.
A mischief in us all lets
light sing and swing.

Honey hushes
the earth's melting. Icicles
winter builds to harden beards
sun melts to water.

My tongue tastes cottony
and I cannot ken mortality
without conjuring a deepening snow.
Words work well in swales.

Heads seek space in spirit.
Deep breaths bring reveries
in hearts pulsing perfect bliss
for hope's song without sorrow.

Stand tall. Breathe air
For prosper of each and all.

# LOVE WORKS

There, summer briars sample air hotter than visitors
Can stand. Buried in the cooler ground
Lies our July. The blistering
Sun sings along with children, hey-diddle diddle, the cat
and the fiddle – fond
Of time they do not understand. There is no moral.
Art is not all nursery rhyme, but a sorrowful
Beauty in atmospheres sharp as a razor.

No one comes to mourn what history sent
Bullying its way to bring the slaves here.
Great-great-grandpap George got caught up in what to do,
then went
Along with the laws. Maybe he was that rare
Master who was good to a fault; how will I ever know
The thicket ahead of my mower now
Will spare more than stones and lichen-etchings.

What belies the bellies in their cramped graves?
Rats, the prowling cat, the waves
The sun slants in salty smears to brave
August on? Today's news fishes for days
When my country will put its money for the right
And leave economics under the starry night
To long for clear and obvious love.

Leave July to sleep with her family.
Let the possum trail for love as it plays dead.
It needs no mere recognition as North America's one
native marsupial.
Its holdings span country and suburbs,

# COW MIRE SONGS

Where the fox and coyote, too, make their dens
For all to see now and then
To aid Love's contrast, Hate, toward extinction.

# About the Author

SHELBY STEPHENSON was the eighth Poet Laureate of North Carolina serving from 2015-1018. He lives on the small farm where he was born near Benson, in the Coastal Plain of North Carolina. "Most of my poems come out of that background," he says, "where memory and imagination play on one another." Educated at the University of North Carolina-Chapel Hill, University of Pittsburgh, and the University of Wisconsin-Madison, he is professor emeritus at the University of North Carolina-Pembroke and served as editor of the international literary journal *Pembroke Magazine* from 1979 until his retirement in 2010. His awards include the Zoe Kincaid Brockman Memorial Award, North Carolina Network Chapbook Prize, Bright Hill Press Chapbook Award, and the Brockman-Campbell Poetry Prize. He has published a poetic documentary *Plankhouse* (with photographs by Roger Manley), plus many chapbooks. *Family Matters: Homage to July, the Slave Girl* won the 2008 Bellday Poetry Prize, and the 2009 Oscar Arnold Young Award. The state of North Carolina presented Shelby with the 2001 North Carolina Award in Literature, and in 2014 he was inducted into the North Carolina Literary Hall of Fame.